MW01152505

Dear _____ ,

_____

_____

From,

_____

'One Day at a Time'

The idea of giving up any addiction for the rest of your life is overwhelming. The good news is that you do not have to do this.

You can approach recovery one day at a time. You don't have to worry about what is going to happen tomorrow or next week.

You just have to get up each morning and commit to staying sober for the rest of the day. By sticking to one day at a time, the days turn into weeks and the weeks turn into years...

The road to recovery is a magical experience but it can also be tough at times. Which is why we rounded up these powerful Addiction Recovery Quotes & Slogans to help you stay motivated.

STAY STRONG!

THE RECOVERY MUST COME FIRST SO THAT EVERYTHING YOU LOVE IN LIFE DOES NOT HAVE TO COME LAST.

ADDICTION IS ALL
ABOUT YOU AND
WHAT YOU WANT.

RECOVERY IS ALL
ABOUT HOW YOU
CAN BE OF HELP
TO OTHERS.

LIVE LESS OUT OF HABIT AND MORE OUT OF INTENT.

ADDICTION IS HIDING
AND DENYING YOUR
FEARS SO AS NOT TO
APPEAR WEAK.

RECOVERY IS
ACKNOWLEDGING
YOUR FEARS AND
LIMITATIONS AND
ASKING FOR HELP.

"I CHOSE
SOBRIETY
BECAUSE I
WANTED A
BETTER LIFE.

I STAY SOBER
BECAUSE I GOT
ONE."

THE SECOND YOU THINK OF GIVING UP, THINK OF THE REASON WHY YOU HELD ON SO LONG.

IT IS NOT GOING TO BE EASY BUT IT IS GOING TO BE WORTH IT.

THERE IS NO SHAME IN BEGINNING AGAIN, IF YOU GET A CHANCE TO BUILD BIGGER AND BETTER THAN BEFORE.

ADDICTION ISN'T ABOUT ALCOHOL AND DRUGS. ITS THE ABSENCE OF SELF. THIS ABSENCE IS DESCRIBED AS A HOLE IN YOUR SOUL. YOU CAN'T LOVE OTHERS WHEN YOU'RE EMPTY INSIDE.

RECOVERY PEELS BACK THE PAINFUL LAYERS AND HEALS THAT HOLE THROUGH HONESTY AND HARD WORK.

TO LOVE ONE SELF IS THE BEGINNING OF A LIFETIME OF RECOVERY.

WHEN YOUR PAST CALLS, DON'T ANSWER.

IT HAS NOTHING NEW TO SAY.

IT DOES NOT MATTER HOW SLOWLY YOU GO AS LONG AS YOU DO NOT STOP.

THE GOAL ISN'T TO BE SOBER. THE GOAL IS TO LOVE YOURSELF SO MUCH THAT YOU DON'T NEED TO DRINK.

"I UNDERSTOOD MYSELF ONLY AFTER I DESTROYED MYSELF. AND ONLY IN THE PROCESS OF FIXING MYSELF, DID I KNOW WHO I REALLY WAS."

RECOVERY IS ABOUT PROGRESSION NOT PERFECTION.

RECOVERY DOESN'T OPEN THE GATES OF HEAVEN AND LET YOU IN.

RECOVERY OPENS THE GATES OF HELL AND LET YOU OUT.

IT'S NOT THAT SOME PEOPLE HAVE WILLPOWER AND SOME DON'T.

IT'S THAT SOME PEOPLE ARE READY TO CHANGE AND OTHERS ARE NOT.

IF YOU FIND YOURSELF IN A HOLE, THE FIRST THING TO DO IS STOP DIGGING.

ADDICTION IS THE DISEASE THAT MAKES YOU TOO SELFISH TO SEE THE HAVOC YOU CREATED OR CARE ABOUT THE PEOPLE WHOSE LIVES YOU HAVE SHATTERED.

RECOVERY IS NOT FOR PEOPLE WHO NEED IT,

IT'S FOR PEOPLE WHO WANT IT.

YOU WERE NEVER CREATED TO LIVE DEPRESSED, DEFEATED, GUILTY, CONDEMNED, ASHAMED OR UNWORTHY.

YOU WERE CREATED TO BE VICTORIOUS.

YOU RATHER GO THROUGH LIFE SOBER, BELIEVING THAT YOU ARE AN ALCOHOLIC, THAN GOING THROUGH LIFE DRUNK, TRYING TO CONVINCE YOURSELF THAT YOU ARE NOT.

YOU DON'T RECOVER FROM ADDICTION ONLY BY STOPPING THE USE.

YOU RECOVER BY CREATING A NEW LIFE WHERE IT'S EASIER TO NOT USE. IF YOU DON'T CREATE A NEW LIFE, THEN ALL THE FACTORS THAT BROUGHT YOU TO YOUR ADDICTION WILL CATCH UP WITH YOU AGAIN.

RECOVERY IS SOMETHING THAT YOU HAVE TO WORK ON EVERY SINGLE DAY AND IT'S SOMETHING THAT DOESN'T GET A DAY OFF.

"I KNOW YOU'RE TIRED, I KNOW YOU FEEL LIKE GIVING UP, BUT YOU'RE NOT GOING TO... YOU KNOW WHY?

BECAUSE YOU ARE STRONG, AND WHEN YOU'VE SURVIVED THROUGH ALL THE SHIT YOUR ADDICTION HAS PUT YOU THROUGH, YOU CAN SURVIVE RECOVERY TOO."

IT'S GONNA GET HARDER BEFORE IT GETS EASIER. BUT IT WILL GET BETTER, YOU JUST GOTTA MAKE IT THROUGH THE HARD STUFF FIRST.

I AM NOT DEFINED BY MY RELAPSES, BUT BY MY DECISION TO REMAIN IN RECOVERY DESPITE THEM.

RECOVERY IS AN ACCEPTANCE THAT YOUR LIFE IS IN SHAMBLES AND YOU HAVE TO CHANGE.

RECOVERY IS A JOURNEY NOT A DESTINATION.

RECOVERY IS HARD, REGRET IS HARDER.

RECOVERY IS NOT A RACE. YOU DON'T HAVE TO FEEL GUILTY IF IT TAKES YOU LONGER THAN YOU THOUGHT IT WOULD.

WHEN YOU CAN STOP,
YOU DON'T WANT TO.
AND WHEN YOU WANT
TO STOP, YOU CAN'T.

THAT'S ADDICTION.

ADDICTION IS A MONSTER;
IT LIVES INSIDE, AND FEEDS OFF
OF YOU, TAKES FROM YOU,
CONTROLS YOU, AND
DESTROYS YOU.

IT IS A BEAST THAT TEARS YOU
APART, RIPS OUT YOUR SOUL,
AND LAUGHS AT YOUR
WEAKNESS. IT IS A STONE
WALL THAT STANDS TO KEEP
YOU IN AND THE REST OUT.

IT IS A SHADOW THAT ALWAYS
LURKS BEHIND YOU, WAITING
TO STRIKE. ADDICTION LIVES
IN EVERYONE'S MIND, SITTING,
STARING, WAITING...

WHEN EVERYTHING SEEMS LIKE AN UPHILL STRUGGLE, JUST THINK OF THE VIEW FROM THE TOP.

PEOPLE ARE NOT ADDICTED TO ALCOHOL OR DRUGS, THEY ARE ADDICTED TO ESCAPING REALITY.

YOU ARE NOT WEAK FOR STRUGGLING. YOU ARE STRONG FOR CONTINUING TO FIGHT.

BE ADDICTED TO IMPROVING YOURSELF.

ADDICTION MAKES YOU BLIND TO YOUR REALITY.

RECOVERY ISN'T ALWAYS EASY, BUT IT CERTAINLY BEATS THE ALTERNATIVE.

"I USED ALCOHOL AND DRUGS TO FEEL BETTER...

I QUIT THEM TO BE BETTER."

IF YOU ARE FACING IN THE RIGHT DIRECTION, ALL YOU HAVE TO DO IS KEEP ON WALKING.

"SOMEONE ONCE TOLD ME, 'I HEARD YOU FINALLY GOT RID OF YOUR ADDICTION.'

I SMILED AND SAID, 'NO, ADDICTION DOESN'T WORK LIKE THAT. ONCE YOU HAVE IT, YOU WILL ALWAYS HAVE IT. I JUST CHOOSE NOT TO FEED IT.'"

HEALING DOESN'T MEAN THE DAMAGE NEVER EXISTED...

IT MEANS THE DAMAGE NO LONGER CONTROLS OUR LIVES.

FOCUS ON WHERE YOU WANT TO GO, NOT WHERE YOU CURRENTLY ARE.

THE BEST TIME TO PLANT A TREE WAS 20 YEARS AGO. THE SECOND BEST TIME IS NOW.

WE DON'T CHOOSE TO BE ADDICTED...

WHAT WE CHOOSE TO DO IS DENY OUR PAIN.

BE STRONGER THAN YOUR STRONGEST EXCUSE.

IT'S A BEAUTIFUL DAY TO BE SOBER.

"NEVER UNDERESTIMATE THE STRENGTH OF A RECOVERING ADDICT...

WE FIGHT FOR OUR LIVES EVERY DAY IN WAYS MOST PEOPLE WILL NEVER UNDERSTAND."

ADDICTION IS THE ONLY PRISON WHERE THE LOCKS ARE ON THE INSIDE.

SOBRIETY IS NOT AN ANCHOR...

IT'S A PAIR OF WINGS.

NOBODY IS IMMUNE FROM ADDICTION...

IT AFFLICTS PEOPLE OF ALL AGES, RACES, CLASSES, AND PROFESSIONS.

ONE STEP AT A TIME.

ONE DAY AT A TIME.

ONE HOUR AT A TIME.

THE CHAINS OF ADDICTION ARE TOO LIGHT TO BE FELT UNTIL THEY ARE TOO STRONG TO BE BROKEN.

AT THE ROOT OF ALL ADDICTION IS PAIN.

ADDICTION IS A FAMILY DISEASE.

ONE PERSON MAY USE, BUT THE WHOLE FAMILY SUFFERS.

ONCE THE ENABLING STOPS, THE RECOVERY IS GIVEN THE OPPORTUNITY TO START.

REMEMBER THAT JUST BECAUSE YOU HIT BOTTOM DOESN'T MEAN YOU HAVE TO STAY THERE.

ROCK BOTTOM IS THE SOLID FOUNDATION ON WHICH YOU CAN REBUILD A BETTER LIFE.

SLOWLY WALKING AWAY FROM HELL IS WHEN YOU START TO GET A GLIMPSE OF HEAVEN.

IT IS THE HARD DAYS THAT MAKE YOU STRONGER.

YOU ARE STRONGER THAN YOU THINK.

THE FIRST STEP IS TO REALIZE THAT YOU ARE WORTH RECOVERY.

STRENGTH DOES NOT COME FROM PHYSICAL CAPACITY.

IT COMES FROM AN INDOMITABLE WILL.

THE EASIEST THING IS TO JUST GIVE UP, BUT TO HOLD IT TOGETHER WHEN EVERYBODY WOULD EXPECT YOU TO FALL APART IS THE TRUE STRENGTH.

COURAGE IS NOT
THE ABSENCE OF
FEAR.

COURAGE IS THE
RESISTANCE TO
FEAR.

COURAGE IS THE
MASTERY OF FEAR.

IT ALWAYS SEEMS IMPOSSIBLE UNTIL IT'S DONE.

IF YOU HEAR A VOICE
WITHIN YOU THAT
SAYS 'YOU CANNOT
DO IT,' THEN BY ALL
MEANS FUCKING DO IT!

AND THAT VOICE WILL
BE SILENCED.

BY CARRYING AWAY SMALL STONES, IT IS NOT IMPOSSIBLE TO MOVE AN ENTIRE MOUNTAIN.

ONLY YOU HAVE THE POWER TO REDEFINE YOUR LIFE & PURPOSE.

USE IT WISELY.

ON THE OTHER SIDE OF FEAR, YOU WILL FIND EVERYTHING YOU'VE EVER WANTED.

ALL OF US PLAY A UNIQUE ROLE IN THE HEALING OF THE WORLD.

SO LET'S DO IT TOGETHER!